Wellness Core Secrets

For Caretakers and Busy Yogi
Professionals

CAROLINA HERRERA
FLÓREZ

BUSY GONE WILD

Your breath, your mind, and your body, on and off the mat. This is for all Yogis who want to learn about the core wellness secrets for your personal ten-minute yoga practice, and have a blast.

CONTENTS

ACKNOWLEDGMENTS

I'm very thankful for all of you readers. May you continue your legendary personal development party and ten-minute yoga blowouts through my books.

"Communicating, moving, and breathing—on and off the mat—is an art of personal living."

Carolina Herrera Flórez, RN Yoga Professional

Bamboozle a System,
Butter Up on Results

Hey, welcome to your ten-minute personal development party and personal yoga blowout reads. I am pleased to have you here. I decided to spill the beans and share all about my wellness core secrets with you. I think this is the next best thing for our personal development party and our ten-minute yoga blowouts. I promise to lay off the scientific jargon, and instead bring you easy and simple reads that you are going to love.

So, let's jump right in.

From a scientific perspective, if there is no system, there are no measurable results. So things, unfortunately, aren't going to fly. Yes, no system means no results. If you didn't systematically approach your personal development parties and yoga blowouts, that is okay—but here is why it is important to go about your ten minutes in a very careful and responsible way. How would you know if those ten minutes are well spent? How do you know if the ten minutes are really working for you? How do you know if those ten minutes of calm and lovely personal yoga or personal development are really effective? And if not, why should you keep that space and practice up? Approaching your ten minutes of personal time in a way that can be measured is golden, for you and for your health.

Results become an analysis of your very own progress. It does not matter if you were only able to sit for one minute or two minutes—guess what? That is a great start!

See, nowadays, we all lead very hectic lives, with a bazillion things to do, with about a thousand thoughts and obligations competing with each other. We all want to know about what is going on with current events, have a presence on social media, spend time with family, exercise, eat healthy, and just about a little bit of everything else. We now have access to all of the information to do these things at our fingertips. Yet, on top of that info—which we wish to feed our brains with more and more each time—we also want to go outside, work, and remain sane.

We have easy access to use and indulge in technology, which is, in my opinion, one of the main drivers to our current busy state. For some of us, putting things on a schedule actually works for tasks to get done. For example, if you are a busy mother/father, or a busy health professional or someone that is responsible for another being, you know that if you aren't present, things don't get done.

So you, my friend, are super-duper important; having a system with some kind of measurable results is the jackpot for your health and overall wellbeing.

Results are the only way to show proof that you are improving or not improving. One of my suggestions for you, the next time you find yourself going to your personal yoga space, is that you find a wearable device that measures stress levels, and measure your stress levels before and after your personal development yoga practice-party. That way, you will see results for yourself.

Core Wellness Secret #1:

Bamboozle Your System

Understand the part of your day that is the one part that you would hate to go on without. For example, for me, it is bathing and brushing my teeth. It took me a while to realize that I take my time with these two lovely self-care rituals. I call bathing and brushing my teeth rituals because I truly enjoy them. So, ask yourself right now and write your answer down. What is the best part of your day?

This is the very first step of your system. Pick a time and commit to that time.

Core Wellness Secret #2:

Groove On, Those Ten Minutes of Personal Yoga

If you know that your system works for you, then it would make a whole lot of sense for you to put this system on repeat and do it over and over again to become really good at it. Groove it, all the way!

Before you started this read, you might never have thought about spending ten minutes of personal yoga accompanying your best part of the day to make things even better. Now, imagine you have your own system to show proof of results—something that makes you feel good and shows that you are getting better and better at focusing on your breath, and therefore your brain and mind are better at focusing all together.

Yay! I'm so excited for you.

For your system, you will always have to:

- Time yourself.

- Describe your experience in three words. These three words will serve as your mantra.

- Mantra in personal yoga: inspiring words for

your own practice.

- Have your space ready for your practice.

Core Wellness Secret #3:

Dance Up on Acceptance

Bring back acceptance into your day, first things first. Okay—you can't make it to a whole sixty minutes of yoga, spinning, or whichever class. Instead, you are creating the best ten minutes of your day—every day—and that is priceless. Accept that a personal development system works for obtaining results that allow you to acknowledge your happy endings, despite the craziness of your everyday life.

In times of stress, we are at risk of going back to old habits. A good idea is to keep track of old bad habits. If a new habit does not spark joy, then move on to a new and better habit. I have worked with many habits myself; often, the simpler you keep things, the better. For example, I know I have to eat my vegetables, right? But when I'm busy, the last thing I really think about grabbing for a bite are vegetables. I've discovered that if I keep small vegetables that I can grab, and enjoy all by themselves, that works for me as opposed to having to come up with some salad alternative that is hard to make and time consuming. Time is of the essence when you are trying to reach goals, so you have to work effectively with what you have and make the most of your time to achieve a certain goal. Sometimes my yoga space is all spiffy, and if I am fully honest, I may never use it. But I do have a mat to practice my Zen in every location of my house. The simpler, the better.

What is scientifically approaching your ten-minute personal development bamboozle? Will this improve your quality of life every day, and will you butter up on results?

The answer means showing up for your ten minutes and jotting down proof of what you did. Over some time, the proof/results through a self-created ten-minute personal system will give you insights, and this is one of the best experiences you will create for yourself. Ever.

As a busy health professional myself, I have to attend to my own needs too. I know how hard this is when you are caring for others and you have work too. For example, little things like going to the bathroom are complicated on busy days. I remember times I spent in hospitals, or on the phone, or at meetings—of course, all really important—yet, I needed my own relief. I remember thinking that it wasn't possible. I had to give a certain medication, or a patient in room six was in pain, or I had to call this peep in one min. I mean, chaos. All around. *I might as well just pee in my pants*, often crossed my mind.

Thankfully, then I was able to recognize elements or people that I would systematically approach for assistance in times of my own personal, physical needs. Ask and I shall receive. With a quick wave, I would ask for help and the situation would be resolved. There are times, friends, when my career and my life kick in full-stress, and I face this big old fact: I have forgotten about my ten minutes that day. Or, simply, I don't have the full energy for anything but to just sit comfortably and work on my pranayama/breathing. I have to accept that fact. There are some days I would love to just sit on my couch, eat popcorn, and watch movies all day long. Those times, when my previous bad habits kick in, I have to allow some time to sort things through and pick myself up again.

So, friend, ten minutes of personal development yoga with acceptance can help you arrange the start, middle, or end of your day, and make that time be thebomb.com.

Disconnect from any device that might be keeping you from enjoying your ten minutes of personal development and focus on your breath with some simple moves. You will find your system, in writing and very organized, so that you can approach and evaluate your practice for results, and feel better and better each time about your practice of breath and movement all together.

Your results are your own evaluation of how things went and what you can improve on. Let's make the most of your time, on and off the mat.

Okay, lets recap:

Core Wellness Secret #1:

Bamboozle Your System - Determine how you will account for your ten minutes and what part of the day.

Core Wellness Secret #2:

Groove On, Those Ten Minutes of Personal Yoga - Time your ten minutes of personal development. Time yourself, have a mantra, and describe your practice in three words.

Core Wellness secret #3:

Dance Up on Acceptance - The fact that you may revert back to old habits in the blink of an eye is something you must plan for. What do you do when stress kicks in and kicks out your new ten-minute personal yoga practice? What is the plan? Acknowledge and accept that stress is bound to happen, and you are going to lose the practice. Go about it with care, give yourself a few days or weeks, and restart again. Always restart. It is never game over. If you are breathing consciously, you can take ten minutes.

Bend Over Your Present

Core Wellness Secret #4:

Your Attitude Is the New Gratitude

Why is attitude important? Here, you are thinking about a lifelong commitment of ten minutes of personal development each day to make happy endings meet and teach your mind, and your brain, about how good this is going to be for you.

The main point is that you have to believe deep within yourself that you can do this, that this is going to work, and that you will be able to stick with this in good times and in bad times; stick with the most awesome personal yoga ten-minute break, even during the days that life breaks you apart.

This is extremely hard to do.

You know you are a human, and the practice of personal development, yoga, and any other exercise form that is enjoyable to you now is a personal, lifelong project. You know you will age and things will be different at every stage.

I recall a story about a customer of mine, Valeria. She was nitty gritty, down on details. Always measuring up to her standards and really working herself hard.

However, Valeria never seemed to reach a certain satisfaction point. She had her practice down, was doing it every day, sharing with others, seeing some progress. But, one day, she shared with me: "Carolina, I keep on being stressed about my numbers; I reach a point where I just don't see any value of showing up for the ten minutes anymore." So, we talked about her three words and mantra, and an effort to come up with gratitude and kindness words for each practice. We didn't talk for a month afterward. The next time I saw her, she had this different look in her eyes. She told me she had been working on her attitude with some gratitude, found new pleasure in buying flowers, kept her apartment clean, and had noticed a lot of new things had started happening to her. This is what I call gratitude for small things; the fact that you are here breathing and reading this, is already pretty cool.

All you can do is support your body by establishing a mindful, regular connection with your awesome-possum brain, mind, and body through the movement of yoga asanas, or personal development exercise of your choice, and have a system that you believe in and recognize how it works for you.

My original aim with yoga was to become a legendary yoga teacher, and then after going through some trainings, I realized, "Well, this does not really resonate with me." But I made the commitment that I would dive into yoga anyway, because I was desperate for tools that I could easily go to, and manage myself. I knew my stress was real, and that my emotional wellness was draining pretty low. I drove myself to trainings, in hopes of information, friendships, and connection with others in many different ways. I was there for other humans when they were sick or needed something, but I was rarely there for myself during those exhausting days.

I know from research studies and other peers that yoga helps with focusing the brain, and helps you be more in tune with how you breathe; modern yoga's ultimate goal is to help us out on our everyday breathing and movements, which ends up benefiting our health. Health, to me, is important. Yes, indeed, ten minutes of your own personal yoga practice means: good health for you and good health for me, ten-minute yogi. So keep practicing, even if you enjoy going to a yoga class. This personal yoga space is much like practice, so you might as well be your own expert at your own breath, to avoid going or not going to an asana or pose unprepared—and you might save a few muscle aches or joint pains. The practice calls for edge, discipline. Let your ten minutes of personal yoga practice be your breakthrough!

Being unprepared is normal, because in yoga, we wear a beginner's hat. We are learning to go to a new pose or move and remain focused on the breath. I remember the first time I tried a headstand. I could barely breathe and I was mostly freaked out about going upside down. I thought I would break my neck, or something horrible would happen. Rest assured, my yoga teacher helped me get there a few times, and it was not until twelve years later in the practice that I could really stand on my head and breathe as if I was standing on my feet.

If you are anything like me, then you realize we did not grow up with the tradition of yoga embedded into our daily lives (if you did, then we are obviously from different areas of the world and you are getting introduced to what modern yoga is starting to shape into). You may have found out about it because someone really cool you know is a yogi, or a studio just opened up next to you, or apps on your phone keep popping up, or YouTube videos show up on your screen. You get it, yoga is everywhere. Everyone recommends it. Practicing the breath along with movement is really good for you. Even if you only get ten minutes every day. Every minute counts.

Let's all remain curious about what yoga is, and see it respectfully as a cultural aspect of the Hindu tradition that provides us with a tool for practicing breathing with movement.

You and I can recognize one simple fact: We seldom have the time to take a breather, or a zenful ten minutes of our own.

Worst, we don't take those ten minutes at all, and this has a bad connotation. When we are stuck in a stressful situation, we either use ten minutes to cool off from the stress, or we stay in the stressful situation all day and never take the time to decompress.

Friends, now is the time. Create your system, plan for results, and check on your attitude with gratitude for those ten minutes. Most importantly, let's have a blast, yogi-friend!

We know one thing is real: Ten minutes of personal yoga practice leaves us refreshed and provides us with the opportunity to move our bodies mindfully.

This is an opportunity that we can give to our bodies to enjoy ten minutes every day. Seize the day!

Best Thing Since Sliced Bread: Your Personal Yoga

Core Wellness Secret # 5:

The Personal Yoga Breath Formula

Simple math:

5 seconds + 5 seconds = 10 seconds

10 seconds * 6 times = 60 seconds

60 seconds = 1 minute

1min = 1 pose/asana

10 poses = your most legendary personal yoga practice

In yoga terms now:

5 seconds to inhale + 5 seconds to exhale = 10 second personal yoga breath

10 second breath * 6 times = 1 personal yoga minute

1 personal yoga minute = you spend on 1 asana or pose

10 asanas/poses = 10 minutes of your most legendary

personal yoga minutes

The formula gets really simple with practice, and you grow with your breath. Oxygen is flowing consciously through your body.

Have a system. Set your timer.

Take your first minute to get in tune with the breath in a grounding position (on the ground).

Be patient.

Be kind.

Attitude is the new Gratitude. Results are what you experience in three words, which eventually will become your mantra—your own inspiring words.

The Breath - Pranayama, in personal yoga, is the oxygen that your blood is capable of catching and bringing to your other organs so they stay functioning. The Pranayama—or life force, you may have heard before—is, in fact, two molecules of Oxygen bound together by a covalent bond and brought to your cells so they don't die and can do their jobs. During Inspiration: you breathe in through your nose, then the breath goes to your lungs, passes through the capillaries, and is picked up by the blood, then carried to your heart and on to the rest of the body. During Expiration: you breathe out, which means the blood came back to the heart from the cells that used up the oxygen; they did some exchanging, and now that oxygen also carries some carbon, which is another type of fuel we humans use to function, so the result of expiration is a release of Carbon with Oxygen. That all happens really quickly. A normal adult at rest should be breathing twelve to twenty times per minute. With our personal yoga breath, we are cutting that rate in half to breath six times in one minute, using five seconds to inhale and five seconds to exhale. Hey, if you ask me, your body totally deserves that kind of break! We humans are wired to work hard without us even knowing it. With personal yoga, too, we go into a pose/asana safely during that one minute. Again, yogi, do not attempt this formula if you think you are not fit for it. Do ask your treating physician or other medical providers if this is the right type of breathing, a type that your body could benefit from. And remember to have lots of fun in the process.

Your Legendary Brain

I promised you I would bring you information that would be easy and simple. So, here it goes. I will do my best.

Core Wellness Secret #6:

Your Brain Is All That and a Bag of Chips

Picture a highway. Now imagine this highway is your nervous system. The nervous system is always fired up and ready to go.

It doesn't really matter how long you have practiced yoga or personal healthcare; the truth is, you will always be a beginner, and there is always something new you have to learn every day.

The brain is an organ, and it weighs about 3lbs, on average, and about 86 billion neurons live there. It is made up of soft tissue and it is contained within the skull at the top of our heads.

The brain is the nervous activity headquarters of our bodies. We know the brain has intellectual capacity, motor coordination capacity, and is also in charge of every function of our bodies.

Some of the brain's main functions include:

- processing sensory information
- regulating blood pressure and breathing
- releasing hormones

Your Legendary Brain and the Nervous System:

The nervous system's job is mainly to transmit signals. So, picture cells with eccentric layers, without movement. These cells are connected and talking to each other about current events that are going on in your body. For example, some of those cells are responsible for catching and responding to the brain's orders given by you. Then, other cells just act on automatic, and you have no power over those parts of your brain.

Usually, nerve cells like to connect and collaborate. Neurons work well together; that is how we are able to move and do things.

The Autonomic Nervous System is a control system. This is our brain's activity, and we are not conscious of it. Our heart rate, digestion, respiratory rate, pupillary response, urination, etc.

As part of the Autonomic Nervous System: The Sympathetic Nervous System is activated by stress and prepares us to fight, and the Parasympathetic Nervous System calms and slows down our response.

The sympathetic nerve cells are more like a funk music band. They are responsible for all the funk you feel when a big old jaguar is chasing you as you cruise through the jungle. You really have no control over this band, other than just thanking them for the loud music while you try to make it alive out of the situation at hand. The parasympathetic nervous system is the one that is responsible for slowing down, and getting you out of that jungle alive.

The Peripheral Nervous System is under our voluntary control. These nerves carry instructions from our brain to our limbs; for example, you being able to move your arms. As well as controlling your muscles and joints, it sends all the information from your senses back to your brain.

Neurons are the basic unit of the brain and nervous system. They are complex cells that live connected with each other. Neurons are specialized cells designed to transmit information to other cells, muscles, or glands.

Knowledge is power; the more you understand how the nervous system works, the more success you will have at enjoying your glow with your flow. As you move through your breath, you are consciously working out the cells that usually work for you automatically. You are bringing in oxygen and moving around energy, which means they also get a bit of a workout.

Evidence tells us that we can dramatically increase the probability of staying mentally and physically fit throughout our lives through physical exercise, good nutrition, social connection with others, and mental stimulation. You are the most important part at ensuring that your brain remains sharp and agile. Start with ten minutes, and you will see for yourself.

The breath is one of those functions that goes under the cells that work on automatic within the sympathetic nervous system. However, you do have control over your breath. Doctors have been studying the pacemaker of our breath for some time: our breath's pacemaker is a cluster of cells that lives on our brain. They've dug further into the genetic makeup of the cells, and what each cell accomplishes. I consider this a bit much to write about, but their work was really important in the world of yoga.

The good news: they support Pranayama, which is that five-second inhale and five-second exhale that relaxes the vagus nerve. The vagus nerve is our longest and most important nerve that resides in the autonomic nervous system. Doctors, and their results, show proof that this personal yoga breath is legit and we can use it to amp up our practice to a new chill, full level of personal yoga and personal development times. Yes! Ten minutes or more of fun, personal flow with yourself in mind.

Your mind is the result of all the work your neurons put out, the brain's ability to hold various functional capacities. Your ability to learn and be conscious, your imagination, your perception, your creativity, your emotions, language, and your memory are all regulated and housed in the brain.

Adding more to the swag, we also know that a daily yoga asana practice will improve your muscle flexibility and strength. This mindful approach to moving your body to your breathing will also increase the awareness of your body; therefore, your posture may improve.

Remember, yoga is a low-impact form of activity for your body and safe when practiced under the guidance of a teacher of your choosing. Always consult with your well-trained yoga teacher before starting a practice. If you have any health concerns, please discuss these with your doctor prior to beginning a daily yoga practice.

Do not use yoga to replace conventional medicine. Always consult with your doctor, and share how many classes you do each week. You should also specify whether it is hot yoga, commercial yoga, YouTube yoga, or better yet, if you are working with a personal trainer or personal yoga teacher. Discuss any benefits or areas of concern, so everyone involved can learn more about your body and treat it safely.

To recap:

Core Wellness Secret #6:

The Highway is your Nervous System, a complex set of cells that will work out as you work out your breath and your body, ten minutes at a time with your personal yoga.

Your Sweetchious Process

Core Wellness Secret #7:

Learn like a Champ

This learning secret is probably the hardest one. I keep saying that wanting to learn is likely the last reason you initially step onto your mat or into your best of breed personal yoga and development party. Really, after a long day of work, all you may want to do is take that nap and go on with your day and spend it elsewhere than with yourself. I get it. I realize getting to this personal space is for heroes. Wow, am I proud of us.

Like with any system that you are creating for yourself, especially one that is so intricate and simple at the same time, such as breath, learning is the only thing that makes a whole lot of sense. Breathing all that oxygen in, and manifesting a state of calm and readiness to take in new information that is valuable to you as a human off your mat and on your mat.

We know that because we lead such busy lifestyles, our attention span has grown a large deficit. So, if you can learn about your own breath, and achieve a certain break, then your mind is ready to learn something new. Your attention span is also getting a bit of exercise too. Staying focused on one thing is hard enough; stretching to stay focused on your breath is even harder.

When your mind is relaxed and focused on the breath, there is really nothing to learn other than to keep the practice going. The learning component always comes after the practice, and it is strictly tied to the results you are wanting to accomplish for yourself.

For example, I struggled with a way to remember how many times I practiced per day, because yes, initially, I did have a whole lot of time and I needed the practice so I could keep up with my learning about yoga. But then I never really tracked any benefit, and I was just worried about sounding right and saying the right words, and just looking pretty and perfect overall. I thought I should be and sound a certain way, but the more I practiced, the more frustrated I felt. Tears of frustration came out, and I never enjoyed teaching yoga. It never felt right. Until that one day, when I realized it is not about being perfect. It is not about sounding a certain way. To me, it is about taking care of the needs at hand. Why do I practice yoga? Because I need a way to relax that is healthy. Why do I need to teach? Because I know that the benefit outweighs the practice, and I have a system that works for me and I am ready to share.

Then, after getting rejected from a few studios, I decided, *Okay, this practice deal has got to get better. I need my own system to practice.* So, I did my best: I stayed off the mat, got an afternoon to spend with my family, and we painted, talked, and ate good food. We listened to music and got our creative hats on. We all worked on this project under my direction, as if we all knew what we where doing. No! I was frustrated, and my family was being super supportive. But, the reality was, I was practicing staying focused on one task, engaging my creative brain and my breath, and decompressing from a self-created situation.

Nothing really came out of that afternoon other than a really pretty picture that I kept up and framed as I pondered on my wellness secrets. *My ten-second breath really helps me with my concentration,* I thought. I had that one down, for sure.

What came after was even better. I now use this picture to help me track how many times I practice every week, for ten weeks.

To recap:

Core Wellness Secret #7:

Learn like a champ! Being a champ at learning will make sense as you show up for your regular ten-minute personal yoga practice.

Your Commitment Shindig

Fantabulous! This is when you decide you are going to practice your personal yoga or personal party every day. This is important because you will see and speak to yourself about this every time you practice: one day at a time.

Much like an Abacus, or a way to measure how much time or how many days you practice, you definitely need clear guidelines so you remain committed:

Core Wellness Secret #8:

Your Commitment Shindig

How to start your commitment revolution:

1. Whizbam a space that you can go to and move freely without any danger in 360 degrees. Entice your senses! Identify your personal favorite and why. Because you need to plan for the best part of your day, ponder the smells, scenery, and music that you like.

2. Identify why you are practicing. Write your three words down. Or, if you can't think of anything, do one word. Every word counts.

Making the most of your ten minutes is probably the best thing you can do for yourself each day.

3. Use online task reminders: Let's face it, breathing on a mat is probably ranked low on your daily to-do list. So, being mindful of a time and creating a commitment to it will serve you the purpose of creating a space for the practice on a busy day. Ensure you are completing the task reminders by giving yourself a completed or not-completed task. Rate yourself.

4. Show up for yourself and then others: It is important to me as your personal yoga teacher that you continue attending other classes. I suggest at least one each week so you can learn from other types of yoga. It is important to establish connections with others and share the practice. Share any feedback on what you do with others.

Major League Zen

Personal yoga is about stretching, moving, and learning. Requesting feedback on successes or failures is really the only way to grow.

Core Wellness Secret #9:

Your Zen Is Spiffylicious

Your application of your idea:

So far you have gone with the flow of this short read. Have a system, plan for results, and understand the personal yoga formula is all about the breath. You are working out the nervous system, your brain and your muscles, and other important organs in your body like your lungs. When you realize this is more like a commitment revolution to the ten minutes of personal yoga or development, you get to create and have a lot of relaxing moments.

Once you are able to put all those pieces together, you will realize you do have the time. You may start giving up those extra ten minutes or unhealthy findings and start checking the boxes on the ten-minute personal yoga calendar reminders.

So far, you have come to realize that ten minutes of personal yoga are amongst the best you can give yourself, especially before you are about to learn something, go out on a presentation, a photo shoot, before a difficult talk with a patient, customer, or client.

Those ten minutes of personal yoga are the bee's knees. And guess what?! You are on your way to enjoying a lifetime habitual practice of them.

Yes, yogi! You are very welcome. I am super excited for you and wish you not only one but a legendary lifetime of wonderful, calm moments that you can recognize every minute you get. Even if it is just one minute. Every minute counts!

Sometimes, you may experience growing pains, such as: *OMG! I have my system in place, and things are all cute and ready to go, yet I only get to spend one minute, or five minutes in my space.* With growth, we do experience growing pains; we may realize there needs to be some tweaking, or some things may need to change, in order for you to get to them.

I used to have this habitual drawing or artsy writing practice after my personal yoga time, and as time progressed and I became busier, as a mother, wife, or professional, I knew I had to make changes, and I knew staying frustrated was not cool. This is why I keep the practice going. I've had to exchange drawing or coloring for daily self-care routines like bathing or brushing my teeth. To this day, I can say my breaths of personal yoga time have helped me overcome stresses and fears, and I have even boosted my own confidence.

One of the things I always remind us of is to understand and perform our yoga as planned, and make any changes that need to happen.

I do encourage the use of personalized devices, only to help tracking and consistency with the result-oriented mentality and living a personal yogic life. Pick a moment of your week or day to log into your fitness device and monitor progress.

Yogi, working your breath, your brain, and your body ain't no easy task. Congratulate yourself for all the successes, and note areas where you can still grow. Ask for guidance or further feedback that will help you continue to improve.

Always check in with your yoga peeps, trainers, and/or medical professionals to make this process work for you.

HAVE FUN IN YOUR PROCESS.

Your Swag and Swank

What I learned during my thirties is that life is happening faster and faster as the years continue. I look back both with some regrets and with no regrets. I feel more and more the need to continue with my ten minutes of personal yoga every time I can. These past two years of sharing some stories and realizing there will always be new ones, I know that growing is an amazing miracle that we are given. These past two years, I've had the pleasure of witnessing weddings, births, and deaths, and such is the cycle of life. We are here for a little bit, then we are not. What we leave is our gains, work, family, and memory.

In my case, I had such an experience of knowing and working with a team of individuals that helped me develop and grow in the form of a writer, health professional, and yogi. Surely, I'm really enjoying this, and I am super excited I get to share with all of you our ten-minute personal development yoga system.

I'm looking forward to the years to come and trust that these ten-minute personal yoga reads will grant me the power and the self-study approach to ensure I continue my aging process gracefully and with the ability to be there for my family, friends, and my profession.

By you joining me and making sure you are also tracking your happy endings and making them meet somewhere along your ten minutes of personal yoga time, you are also starting to realize that, while we are here only for a bit, we can still make the most out of it, and it does not take much other than staying in tune with our breath and our being. Then, adding a bit of movement and purpose to why you want to keep this personal practice going.

What is the real gain for understanding and acting on the breath and the brain for your day?

Think now—every day, every year. You will realize you grew a little, because it is inevitable. For, as age always goes up, so your wisdom, your practice, and your breath should also be going in that direction. Why not? What have you got to lose? Nothing! And you have all the gains to gain.

My stories all draw many parallels to yoga. Yoga looks fun and yoga teachers move with such ease, standing on their heads and twisting like pretzels. Their bodies seem healthy and easy to handle. As you step onto the mat, you probably think that the last thing you are there to do is to learn about you. As the class starts, the yoga teacher begins talking and kindly guiding the asanas, and suddenly everyone is moving and breathing. The result is beautiful. Everyone is in dance with their bodies, engaged in thoughts, or trying to disengage from thoughts and focusing on whatever the practice brings to them—hopefully some real-time lessons about their breathing. After the practice, or during the practice, you look back and you analyze how you were able or not able to connect your mind, breath, and movement.

This is hard to do, but with practice and dedication, anything is possible. As a child, I learned that I wanted to be able to move and travel, and to this day, I am grateful I chose to travel at a young age. As an adult, I am thankful to the idea of learning and being committed to learning, so I can experience growth. Your personal yoga practice teaches you about yourself. Relax and enjoy, while you are here committing to grow your personal yoga, ten minutes at a time.

This chapter has no secret. We know age is inevitable. You have the power to live your healthiest life, one personal yoga breath at a time. One growing pain at a time. One happy ending at a time. Learn to recognize your pains, your gains, and your growth, and aging might come along as a friend.

110 Percent in Progress

It is easier to adapt when we are younger. As the years go by, comfort starts to set in and we get set in our ways. During my thirties, I've worked really hard, I've graduated from a few schools, and now I find myself living in the sweet comfort zone—that zone in which I sit and life is beautiful and days go by.

I often find myself thinking back to my earlier times, in my thirties, twenties, or teens. Times in which energy never ceased and every day took forever— time was not of the essence. If you ask me, as we age, things happen faster. Awareness and wisdom start to take shape in your days, and fear comes along for a visit every so often.

About a year ago, I wrote *Learn, Commit, Grow: With Personal Yoga*. My first three words, I got to practice all year round. Boys and girls, was I scared—I had no clue as to what I was doing. I just knew those ten minutes really work for me and was hopeful to share with others. Thankful for the support I received, I launched a book and had a celebration; friends came by and we celebrated an accomplishment. Together.

Fast-track to my *Wellness Core Secrets*, my three new

words I keep close and cherish like a Ferrari, or some really cool, artistic, one-of-a-kind vehicle that transforms my everyday living into a happy moment. The new three words serve me as a powerful mantra as my aging continues. I get to share with you once again, with more confidence, and clear results that this practice is effective and proven to work.

A source from within. A creation of my own. A piece of art. Words sticking together with a powerful message. A work that will always be a work in progress.

Core Wellness Secret #10:

You Are Never Really Off the Hook

In health and in yoga, your work is always a work in progress.

I always find that it is important to understand why staying committed to something is worth the time, the hardship, and the effort. To me, it is really important to give back, and be a part of the personal yoga revolution ten minutes at a time.

I hope to continue to train myself to be flexible, adapt to change, and learn as much as I can from experiences to adapt accordingly. Breathing is the kind act that we humans do to our bodies so they stay functioning. Oxygen is our source of energy to live. If you are breathing, you are alive. Yoga is a tradition, that I will continue to respect and adapt to our modern world in a way that works.

Personal yoga is about breathing. It is about moving your body with your breath. This simple act of getting and staying committed to a practice or a hobby is worth the effort.

Brute Force It with Technology and Personal Yoga

I've discovered powerful commands: in technology, "Alexa, set timer, ten minutes"; "Alexa, enable forest sounds"; in personal yoga, "Carolina, breathe."

Let's continue the discussion about virtual yoga and how we are here. When I started learning about yoga informally, I would have never guessed that I would stretch myself to teach yoga and share knowledge. I tried teaching at yoga studios and private classes, and I did not like it. Initially, I only went to classes for my own benefit. I started taking yoga classes as the new form of fitness that was slowly growing in my community. Yoga continues to be that feel-good sport I practice after my biking, hiking, running, walking, and skating.

I practice, and the more I practice, the better I get. At yoga, with my breath, vo2 max improved, and stress levels have lowered dramatically. I enjoy writing, sharing messages, and I've met some really awesome people in the process.

I've learned much more than yoga; this practice has stretched my brain into directions I never thought or imagined I would steer into.

I find this fascinating. I really hope you and I get to work on our writing and reading about health and yoga together forever!

As we always wear so many hats during our days, let's find balance, beauty, and purpose, and always aim for the enjoyment of our growth as our days go by.

I know that with my passion for health and wellness, I am ready to continue that commitment to my personal yoga fun time, and I am truly pleased that I get to share with you too.

I am ready to merge yoga and wellness, and to serve all of you looking to incorporate some personal, safe yoga into their day.

The perspective of being free to practice at the times it is convenient for myself, depending on the day, and understanding why we lead a practice and why I lead others to create their personal practice entices me. Together, we can work on our brains, our health, and our calm, and live in a frantic world, one shared breath at a time.

With my words and experiences, I invite you to continue your work with reading, watching videos, going to classes, and talking about how a ten-minute personal yoga practice can support your day. Teach yoga, if that is your calling!

A special thanks for all the support I continue to receive while writing, and for the inspiration from all of you yogis. This book, my work, and my dedication are for you.

Dear caregivers and busy yogi professionals, thank you for reading. I am so happy you are here, and wish you nothing but the best. To recap on all the secrets:

Core Wellness Secret #1: Bamboozle Your System

Core Wellness Secret #2: Groove On, Those Ten Minutes of Personal Yoga

Core Wellness Secret #3: Dance Up on Acceptance

Core Wellness Secret #4: Your Attitude Is the New Gratitude

Core Wellness Secret #5: The Personal Yoga Breath Formula

Core Wellness Secret #6: Your Brain Is All That and a Bag of Chips

Core Wellness Secret #7: Learn like a Champ

Core Wellness Secret #8: Your Commitment Shindig

Core Wellness Secret #9: Your Zen Is Spiffylicious

Core Wellness Secret #10: You Are Never Really Off the Hook

Namaste.

ABOUT THE AUTHOR

Carolina approaches yoga as her personal time to explore breathing, moving, and establish a connection between her mind and body. She is known for her authentic, non-judgmental teaching style and her compassion-centered philosophy. She encourages a safe yoga practice by working with a simple routine. For Carolina, yoga is a tool that helps her learn at her own pace about working the body. She defines moving and breathing as very powerful tools when leading a healthy and balanced lifestyle.